BOOKS OF THE OLD TESTAMENT

FOR CHILDREN

Written by Julianne Booth
Illustrated by Art Kirchhoff

ARCH® Books

Copyright © 1981 CONCORDIA PUBLISHING HOUSE,
ST. LOUIS, MISSOURI
MANUFACTURED IN THE UNITED STATES OF AMERICA
ALL RIGHTS RESERVED
ISBN 0-570-06151-2

The Bible's first book is GENESIS.
 You'll find when you begin it,
It tells of how God made the world
 And all the creatures in it.
This book is full of wonderful tales
 Of the time when the world was new,
Of Adam and Eve in their garden,
 And Noah's great floating zoo.
Then we read of Father Abraham,
 Who crossed the desert sand.
He answered God's call and left his home
 To seek the Promised Land.
Isaac and Jacob and Jacob's twelve sons—
 We watch generations roll by,
Branches on Abraham's family tree,
Who would someday be more than the sands of the sea,
 And more than the stars of the sky.
From them, we read, would come someday
The Savior who takes our sins away.

In EXODUS we learn of Moses,
　　A baby saved from the Nile.
He grew up as a prince of Egypt,
　　Though his people were slaves all the while.
But God had a plan for Moses
　　To free the Hebrews—so,
He sent him to plead at Pharaoh's court:
　　"Let my people go!"
With signs and wonders and mighty acts
　　God led His people out.
Through stormy sea and wilderness,
　　We hear their excited shout!
On to Mount Sinai they came,
God's holy mountain of mighty fame.
There Moses went up to learn God's law.
When he came down again, what a sight he saw!
His people worshiped a calf of gold!
Moses was angry and had to scold!

The next book is LEVITICUS.
　　It's full of information
On laws revealed from God on high
　　To govern the Hebrew nation.

The Book of NUMBERS gets its name
　　Because with figures it abounds.
When Moses took a census count,
　　He wrote the people's numbers down.

And then when Moses' death drew near,
He called the tribes that they might hear
A grand review of all he'd taught,
And how to do God's will he'd sought.
Where can we read this parting speech?
    The answer I will tell:
In DEUTERONOMY, the book
    Of Moses' last farewell.

Then Moses' friend JOSHUA took command
And brought the tribes to the Promised Land.
A warrior bold, of iron will,
He fought his foes while the sun stood still.
And all have heard of his great renown,
When Jericho's walls came tumbling down.

But after Joshua had died
Enemies humbled Israel's pride.
So God sent JUDGES to guide the land,
To lead His people and take command.
Deborah, Gideon, Samson too,
Tried their best to serve Him true.

Meanwhile in the town of Bethlehem
    There lived a young woman named RUTH
Who believed in the God of Israel
    And followed His path of truth.

The long book of FIRST SAMUEL,
    With thirty-one chapters in all,
Tells of Samuel, the last of the judges,
    And his troubles with King Saul.

SECOND SAMUEL is strangely named,
  For really this is the part
Of the Bible that tells of King David,
  A man after God's own heart.

Then Solomon, King David's son,
Ruled when David's reign was done.
The book of FIRST KINGS tells the story
Of Solomon in all his glory.
Later kings, too, in this book belong,
Some good, some bad, some weak, some strong.

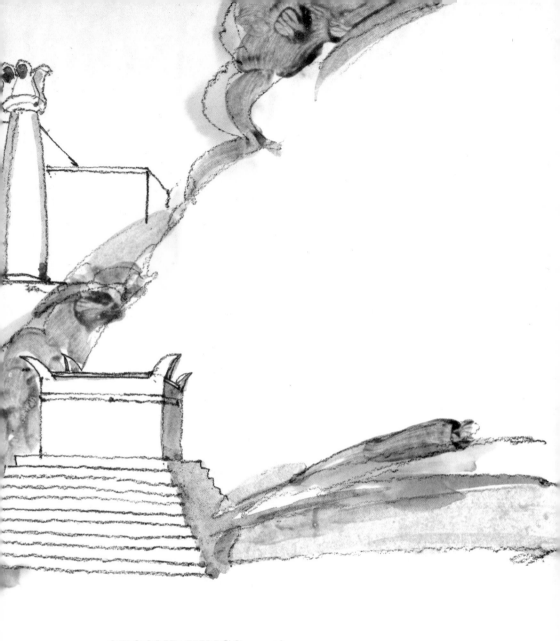

SECOND KINGS continues on
To the time when all the kings were gone.
Samaria fell, and Jerusalem too,
But the history of Israel is far from through!

FIRST and SECOND CHRONICLES
Retell old Israel's story,
Compiled, at God's urging, by a scribe
To review his nation's glory.

Then EZRA came from Babylon,
    A scholar wise was he.
He read his scrolls at the Water Gate
And told his people, "It's not too late
    To serve God more faithfully."

And NEHEMIAH built a wall
　　　For old Jerusalem town.
His foes tried to stop him, but he replied,
　　　"I'm working! I cannot come down!"

In Persia, Queen ESTHER, lovely and brave,
Risked her life her people to save.

16

JOB is a story of suffering,
  Of a worthy man and true,
Who lost his wealth, and lost his health,
  And all his children too.
But God was kind, and by His plan
Job ended up a happy man.

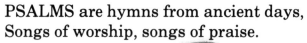

PSALMS are hymns from ancient days,
Songs of worship, songs of praise.

The Book of PROVERBS, you will find,
Contains wise words of many a kind.

ECCLESIASTES has wisdom too;
Here's a quote, both wise and true:
"What has been done is what will be done.
There is nothing new under the sun."

The SONG OF SOLOMON, Song of Songs,
   Tells of the gift of love.
It may be the love of man and wife,
   Or the mercy of God above.

Next come the prophets, men who were sent
To proclaim God's message wherever they went.
Led by God's Spirit, wise words they did teach,
And oft' of the coming Messiah they'd preach.

ISAIAH saw a vision of God,
    And much afraid was he,
But he knew that he'd been called to serve,
    And he said, "Here I am! Send me!"
And God let Isaiah clearly see
The Savior who'd suffer for you and for me.

JEREMIAH lived in troubled times
  And often spoke of gloom.
His words were sad, but he was right
  When he foretold his nation's doom.

The LAMENTATIONS next record
  Jerusalem's tragic fall.
Jeremiah's predictions indeed came true,
  Though none had believed him at all.

While EZEKIEL of Babylon watched the skies,
Strange visions appeared before his eyes,
Hovering wheels, like U. F. O.'s,
And what they were, nobody knows.
But God can work in mysterious ways,
And so did Ezekiel, all his days.

The Book of DANIEL, an ancient writing,
Is full of adventures most exciting!
Fiery furnace and lions' den
Prove no peril when angels step in!

HOSEA tells of the love of his life,
Faithless Gomer, his wandering wife.

In the days of JOEL a locust swarm
Covered the land and caused great harm.

AMOS the herdsman came to town
And pleaded, "Let justice like waters roll down."

OBADIAH speaks of the Edomites.
　　His book is the shortest one,
Only one chapter, "Edom will fall,"
　　He declared, Then his work was done.

JONAH wanted to hide from God,
　　But he found God is everywhere.
Though he tried to flee,
In the depths of the sea
　　He learned of God's loving care.

"Do justice and love mercy,
  And walk humbly with your God."
These are the words of MICAH,
  And such was the path he trod.

"Wasted is Nineveh," NAHUM declared,
And Judah rejoiced while their foes despaired.

HABAKKUK on his tower
Looked out across the land.
"O Lord, how long," he wondered,
"Our troubles must we stand?"

ZEPHANIAH preached of judgment day
And urged us all to seek God's way.

HAGGAI and ZECHARIAH
Lived in Judah's later days.
They helped build the Second Temple,
And for this they win our praise.

Last of all comes MALACHI,
The messenger of the Lord.
"One God and Father made us all,"
This prophet does record.

Thus in thirty-nine books from days of old
Many a wonderful story is told.
On every page of the Bible we see
That God cares for His people, for you and for me.
And all of it's written, by God's inspiration,
To point us to Jesus and His salvation.
For God promised to send, we read in His Word,
Jesus our Friend, our Redeemer and Lord.

Dear Parents,

The drama unfolded in the Old Testament is not merely the story of a small nation in the ancient Near East that boasts of a colorful history. It is our story too, as sons and daughters created in God's image for communion with Him. Like Old Testament Israel, our lives are also marred by sin and indifference to God, but nevertheless He continues to reach out to us in grace and forgiveness as He did to His chosen people long ago.

The books of the Old Testament trace the progression and development of that promise as it led to fulfillment in Jesus Christ, God's Son, the Messiah foretold in the Old Testament to bear the guilt and punishment that Israel then and you and I today deserve. "For to us a child is born, to us a son is given; . . . and His name will be called 'Wonderful Counselor, Mighty God, Everlasting Father, Prince of Peace'" (Isaiah 9:6).

As you read this book with your child, emphasize the great love God had for His people then and the love He continues to shower on us each day. Enjoy your journey through the Old Testament!

The Editor